# ANGELIQUE STARKEY
# COLLECTION OF POEMS

ANGIE STARKEY

**Gotham Books**

30 N Gould St.
Ste. 20820, Sheridan, WY 82801
https://gothambooksinc.com/

Phone: 1 (307) 464-7800

© 2023 Angelique Starkey. All rights reserved.

No part of this book may be reproduced, stored in a retrieval system, or transmitted by any means without the written permission of the author.

Published by Gotham Books (May 5, 2023)

ISBN: 979-8-88775-102-3 (sc)
ISBN: 979-8-88775-103-0 (e)

Because of the dynamic nature of the Internet, any web addresses or links contained in this book may have changed since publication and may no longer be valid.

The views expressed in this work are solely those of the author and do not necessarily reflect the views of the publisher, and the publisher hereby disclaims any responsibility for them.

# Table of Contents

Dedication Page ................................................ 21
About the Author .............................................. 23
Beautiful Tree ................................................... 25
Husband .......................................................... 26
My Children ..................................................... 27
Wild Child ........................................................ 28
Mother Nature Roar's ........................................ 29
Return Home .................................................... 30
Problems .......................................................... 31
Mission ............................................................. 32
Dog's and Cats .................................................. 33
To Nite ............................................................. 34
Work is done .................................................... 35
THANK THE HEAVEN ..................................... 36
I'm Older ......................................................... 37
One of a Kind ................................................... 38
I Met You ......................................................... 39
Fate .................................................................. 40
Tender Touch ................................................... 41
Be mine ............................................................ 42

| | |
|---|---:|
| *Your Flame* | 43 |
| *Make it Through* | 44 |
| *As The Thunder Roar's* | 45 |
| *The Breakup* | 46 |
| *As I Get Older* | 47 |
| *Surrender* | 48 |
| *Me And You* | 49 |
| *I Will Be Around* | 50 |
| *Darkness Bound* | 51 |
| *Thrive* | 52 |
| *Wait* | 53 |
| *Hearts Rest* | 54 |
| *If I Didn't Have You* | 55 |
| *Water's* | 56 |
| *Proceed to Write* | 57 |
| *Unknown* | 58 |
| *A Blast* | 59 |
| *Dance Around* | 60 |
| *Wrath* | 61 |
| *Don't Lose Your Light* | 62 |
| *God's Light* | 63 |
| *My Van* | 64 |
| *Girl Of My Dreams* | 65 |
| *Soak My Feet* | 66 |
| *Unplanned* | 67 |

| | |
|---|---|
| Sky's | 68 |
| Misread | 69 |
| Beans | 70 |
| This Book | 71 |
| Lacey | 72 |
| Easter Bunny | 73 |
| Grandchildren | 74 |
| Blessed | 75 |
| Story Told | 76 |
| Lighthouse | 77 |
| Love Flows | 78 |
| Paradise | 79 |
| The Dark | 80 |
| Honey's Bear's | 81 |
| Mother's Love | 82 |
| Nimm | 83 |
| Paisley's Paws | 84 |
| A Hurricane | 85 |
| Keep You Near | 86 |
| Ukraine War | 87 |
| His Light | 88 |
| Left To Die | 89 |
| A Better World | 90 |
| Ground Round | 91 |
| Better Life | 92 |

| | |
|---|---|
| Harmony | 93 |
| Youthful Days | 94 |
| Fly Free | 95 |
| Home of My Own | 96 |
| Flowers | 97 |
| We Were Young | 98 |
| Hoping To Mend | 99 |
| Say | 100 |
| Zena | 101 |
| So Long | 102 |
| This Book | 103 |
| My Little Dog | 104 |
| Pure Bliss | 105 |
| My Dogs | 106 |
| Let's Mend | 107 |
| Wallet | 108 |
| The Cat | 109 |
| Wolves Call | 110 |
| Wolves Howl | 111 |
| As Darkness Falls | 112 |
| Enter Peace | 113 |
| Bird Song | 114 |
| Heavenly Life | 115 |
| Date | 116 |
| Summer Day | 117 |

| | |
|---|---|
| Shed of Light | 118 |
| Tornado | 119 |
| Fiery Love | 120 |
| Massive storms | 121 |
| Living my Dream | 122 |
| Chicken Meal | 123 |
| Excuse Me | 124 |
| Animals of Nature | 125 |
| A Glance | 126 |
| Open Range | 127 |
| Sincere | 128 |
| Home Alaska | 129 |
| Night Away | 130 |
| Stars Aline | 131 |
| Mountain Top | 132 |
| America | 133 |
| Beautiful World | 134 |
| Ton's of Fun | 135 |
| The Eagle | 136 |
| Animals | 137 |
| More Than | 138 |
| A New Start | 139 |
| A Whisper | 140 |
| You're The One | 141 |
| Companion | 142 |

| | |
|---|---|
| Belong | 143 |
| Compassion | 144 |
| Sleep Tight | 145 |
| Rain's | 146 |
| Close To You | 147 |
| Seagull | 148 |
| Prowl | 149 |
| Time To Change | 150 |
| Cocoa | 151 |
| Good Live's | 152 |
| Shine On | 153 |
| Candle | 154 |
| The Sun | 155 |
| Dancer | 156 |
| Wood Stove | 157 |
| Gone | 158 |
| Our Mind | 159 |
| A Rose | 160 |
| Never Part | 161 |
| Summer Storms | 162 |
| Mosquitos | 163 |
| Smile | 164 |
| Lightning Flash | 165 |
| Heart Is True | 166 |
| Love | 167 |

| | |
|---|---|
| Peace And Beauty | 168 |
| Find Love | 169 |
| Precious Time | 170 |
| Rise Up | 171 |
| Cool Breeze | 172 |
| The Will | 173 |
| In My Life | 174 |
| Forever | 175 |
| Favorite Songs | 176 |
| My Devotion | 177 |
| Blessed | 178 |
| It's Okay | 179 |
| Good Bye | 180 |
| Depression | 181 |
| Greatest Love | 182 |
| Mermaid | 183 |
| Days Pass On | 184 |
| Glow Of Light | 185 |
| The Place | 186 |
| Smell Of Rain | 187 |
| A Little Bark | 188 |
| Son | 189 |
| Shelter Animal | 190 |
| As You Cry | 191 |
| Voice Roar | 192 |

Love Is Bright..................................................... 193
I Will Be The One................................................ 194
Run..................................................................... 195
Poems................................................................ 196
All Time.............................................................. 197
Gleam................................................................. 198
Pass You By....................................................... 199
Follow Your Dreams........................................... 200
Being Blue......................................................... 201
Smile Bright....................................................... 202
Except Me.......................................................... 203
I Need You......................................................... 204
Never Blue......................................................... 205
Mend.................................................................. 206
Another Life....................................................... 207
Separate Ways.................................................. 208
Remember......................................................... 209
On The Street.................................................... 210
I'm Here............................................................. 211
Kind A Cold....................................................... 212
On My Knee's.................................................... 213
I'm Poor............................................................. 214
My Clock........................................................... 215
Times Of War.................................................... 216
Cooking Pot...................................................... 217

| | |
|---|---|
| Better Day | 218 |
| Flashlight | 219 |
| Embrace | 220 |
| Pop Bottle's | 221 |
| A Mess | 222 |
| Share Our Life | 223 |
| A Hole | 224 |
| Always Love | 225 |
| Gravity | 226 |
| Picnic | 227 |
| Work | 228 |
| Summer Sun | 229 |
| Having Fun | 230 |
| rBreaking Hearts | 231 |
| Out Of Gas | 232 |
| United States | 233 |
| Heart Ache | 234 |
| A Good Man | 235 |
| Recognize | 236 |
| Soldier | 237 |
| Married | 238 |
| Fire | 239 |
| Typhoon | 240 |
| God Is Great | 241 |
| My Story | 242 |

| | |
|---|---|
| Dawn's Light | 243 |
| Floods | 244 |
| Show Me Lord | 245 |
| Another Tomorrow | 246 |
| Share Memories | 247 |
| Heaven Sent | 248 |
| Best Love | 249 |
| Every Step | 250 |
| A Plan | 251 |
| Super Hero | 252 |
| River Of Love | 253 |
| Beautiful Lands | 254 |
| Hold On | 255 |
| Love Is a Storm | 256 |
| As You Walked By | 257 |
| Beauty We Hold | 258 |
| Live Wire | 259 |
| Sweet Story | 260 |
| Forever Stand | 261 |
| White Owl | 262 |
| Lonely Lover | 263 |
| Dark Clouds | 264 |
| Heart Of Gold | 265 |
| Morning Dew | 266 |
| On My Feet | 267 |

| | |
|---|---|
| Next To Me | 268 |
| Hush Puppy | 269 |
| Love Will Grow | 270 |
| Rain Drops | 271 |
| Floods Draw Near | 272 |
| Lightning Strikes | 273 |
| Have Fun | 274 |
| Grow | 275 |
| Teddy Bear | 276 |
| The Dawn's Light | 277 |
| Alaska The Place | 278 |
| Games And Lies | 279 |
| Sunsets | 280 |
| Snow Fall | 281 |
| Move To the Beat | 282 |
| Love Flows Free | 283 |
| Poodle Puppy | 284 |
| A Lot Better | 285 |
| Celtic Music | 286 |
| The Sun | 287 |
| Dreams Don't Die | 288 |
| God's Work | 289 |
| Aurora Lights | 290 |
| Our Life | 291 |
| Motion | 292 |

See Threw ............................................................ 293
Don't Walk Away ................................................ 294
Stay ..................................................................... 295
Salmon ................................................................ 296
I Pray .................................................................. 297
Angelique's .......................................................... 298
Glorify ................................................................. 299
So Bold ................................................................ 300
Better .................................................................. 301
I Cry .................................................................... 302
Pretty Eye's ......................................................... 303
Dust From A Star ................................................ 304
Cauldron .............................................................. 305
A Soldier's Storm ................................................ 306
Ghouls Of The Night ........................................... 307
Dreaming On A Star ............................................ 308
Freedom Forever ................................................ 309
Worth .................................................................. 310
You To Hold ........................................................ 311
Dance Around ..................................................... 312
North Star ........................................................... 313
Splashed .............................................................. 314
I Lost You ............................................................ 315
Rock Star ............................................................. 316
I Survive .............................................................. 317

| | |
|---|---|
| Clam's | 318 |
| Try | 319 |
| Clam's | 320 |
| A Dove | 321 |
| Gold Dust | 322 |
| Furry Friend | 323 |
| Fire Flies | 324 |
| She | 325 |
| Spring | 326 |
| Haley's Comet | 327 |
| Harp | 328 |
| No Nuclear War | 329 |
| Dice | 330 |
| The Lord Loves Us | 331 |
| Day We Met | 332 |
| The Witch | 333 |
| Talking To You | 334 |
| Never Broken | 335 |
| Shall Pass | 336 |
| God Walks Beside Me | 337 |
| White Red and Blue | 338 |
| A Child's Smile | 339 |
| Clover | 340 |
| River of Gold | 341 |
| Glacier Water | 342 |

Treasure of Gold ....................................................... 343
Worth ........................................................................ 344
The Witch .................................................................. 345
Heavy ........................................................................ 346
Forget Me Not ........................................................... 347
A Soldier's Storm ...................................................... 348
I Pray ........................................................................ 349
Showing Beauty and Love ........................................ 350
My Devotion .............................................................. 351
SHE ........................................................................... 352
Talking To You .......................................................... 353
I Cry .......................................................................... 354
WORTH ..................................................................... 355

# Dedication Page

*I would like the book dedicated to my children......*

*Lacey.......Ashley......Joshua........Jessica.*

## About the Author

*Born October 1968 loves nature loves animals' lives in Happy Valley Alaska loves open Skies and wildflowers being one with nature helped me write my poems I hope you like them.*

# Beautiful Tree

A Beautiful Tree
That I Planted from
A Seed for The Birds and Bee's
Bless it Be

# Husband

*When You Get home
You won't Be Alone
Your Husband so True
I Love You*

# My Children

My children
I miss talking to You
I love to hear Your voice
Now Your older
And You have Your own choice
You've decided to move on
You have a family and life of your own
But I still love and miss You
Even when your gone
Love Your mom
**Dedicated To:** My Children

# Wild Child

*Your A wild child*
*With A Beautiful Style*
*And A Pretty Smile*

# Mother Nature Roar's

Mother Nature Roar's
Bringing with Her
Tornado's That Soar
Tsunami's That wash upon The Shore's
She Brings massive waves
She is The one To Blame
She Floods Across THE Plains
And Doe's it with out shame
She Doesn't Hide
As She cause's Her Land Slides
Her And Her Friend Climate Change
Will Rearrange

# Return Home

I Hate To Be Gone
I don't Like To Leave You Alone
My days Seem To Be Really Long
I Can't wait until I Return Home

# Problems

You've Got Problems  
And I've Got mine  
Let's Take Time  
And Find A way  
To Help One Another  
And Be Kind

# Mission

*I'm on A mission*
*As I follow my intuition*
*And Now I can clearly see*
*That it's There Right in Front of me*
*OH, Bless it Be*

# Dog's and Cats

*Some Dogs And Cats Across The Land*
*Are very sad*
*They Don't want To Be Alone or cold*
*They want someone To Hold*
*And Given a Good Home*

# To Nite

To Nite
Your Love Shines Brite
You make me Feel All Right
Under The moon Lite

# Work is done

From Beginning To End
My work is Done
I Had Fun
Writing These
I Hope You Are
Pleased

# THANK THE HEAVEN

*I THANK THE
Heaven Above
That God Gave Me
Someone To Love*

# I'm Older

Now I'm older
I'm Not As Young As I Once was
I Have Age Spots from The Sun
But I Still Thrive
And I Feel Alive
And I Still Go on with Life
Because I Know I'm Still
Beautiful on The Inside

# One of a Kind

Eye's as blue
As the deep blue sea
A smile you would love
To see
Long beautiful hair
That would shine
She was one of a kind
I wish she was mine

# I Met You

Before I met You
My world was blue
Unhappy and sad
And lonely to
But now I'm happy as can be
And dancing on dream

# Fate

*Fate brought us together*
*So soft and tender*
*The love you have*
*Given me*
*Couldn't be any better*

# Tender Touch

*Your touch is so soft and tender*
*That I surrender*
*And I will always remember*
*Your soft and tender touch*
*I love you so much*

# Be mine

*Like sands of time*
*Like stars in the sky*
*You will always be mine*
*Until the end of*
*Time*

# *Your Flame*

I see You and my heart
Started pounding
It felt like I was
Drowning
I need to know Your name
I want to be your flame

# Make it Through

*Forever true*
*My heart belongs to you*
*Through good times*
*Or bad*
*We will always*
*Make it through.*

# As The Thunder Roar's

As I sit and wonder
I start to hear the sounds of thunder
As I open up my door
It starts to pour
I hurry and shut my door
As the thunder roar's

# The Breakup

*You once were loved*
*You brought joy and laughter*
*Like warmth from the sun*
*I will always have good memories*
*When we were as one*
*I'm sad your gone*
*But You've decided to move on*

# As I Get Older

As I get Older
I know my time in this world will get shorter
I not scared to leave
I just wanna keep live in my dream

# Surrender

*Surrender Your love*
*Hear my call*
*We could have it*
*All*

# Me And You

We got married young
Me and You
Then we had a baby
And our child grew
We stayed together
For Seventy Years
Me and You
And we loved one another
Forever true

## I Will Be Around

*When your feeling down*
*I will be around*
*To sooth and console*
*And help*
*Heal Your soul*

# Darkness Bound

As I listen to the sounds
Of the shrilling hoot owl
In the distance I hear
The battle cries of the wolf's howl
I am in the doubt
Darkness Bound

# Thrive

*Don't close your eyes*
*Look at your beautiful life*
*So strive and you*
*Will thrive*

# Wait

*I hate to sit and wait*
*On my date*
*But it's better late*
*Then never*

# Hearts Rest

*Let's, let our hearts*
*Rest*
*I wish You the best*

# If I Didn't Have You

My world would be blue
My heart broken in two
I wouldn't have a clue
On what to do
If I didn't have You

# Water's

*God gave us water's
Upon the Earth
So, the people don't thirst*

# Proceed to Write

*As you read the words that I write*
*About some things that happen in my life*
*I hope you like my poems and smile bright*
*And I will hold my head up tight*
*And proceed to write*

# Unknown

*Somewhere unknown*
*My life will be*
*told*

# *A Blast*

I wish summer would last
I don't want it to pass
I've had a blast
Running and playing
Outside on the grass

# Dance Around

I dance around
And listen to the sound
Of music I love to hear
And I yell and cheer

# Wrath

*It is sad*
*But the wrath of mother nature*
*Is at hand*
*Across the land*
*I feel bad*
*But its mother nature's*
*Demand*

# Don't Lose Your Light

*Through the Rough and bad*
*I will hold your hand*
*Don't lose your light*
*You still have life*
*Put up a fight*

# God's Light

God's light
Shines so bright
He gives us the moon
To live by night

# My Van

*I'm a happy man*
*Driving my van*
*Across the land*

# Girl Of My Dreams

When I first saw You
I just couldn't believe
I tripped over my own feet
Oh Lord how could It be
The girl of my dreams
Just smiled at me

# Soak My Feet

*Tired and Beat*
*I love the Heat*
*As I soak my feet*

# Unplanned

*It was unplanned*
*But hear we stand*
*So, I took your Hand*
*As we listened to the band*

# Sky's

*The bird's eye's
Look upon the beautiful sky's
As they fly*

# Misread

*It stuck in my head*
*When I read*
*The words you said*
*I felt dread*
*Whoops I'm sorry*
*I misread*

# Beans

*A little Bit of*
*Beef stock*
*Added to my pot*
*Of Bean's and*
*HamHock*

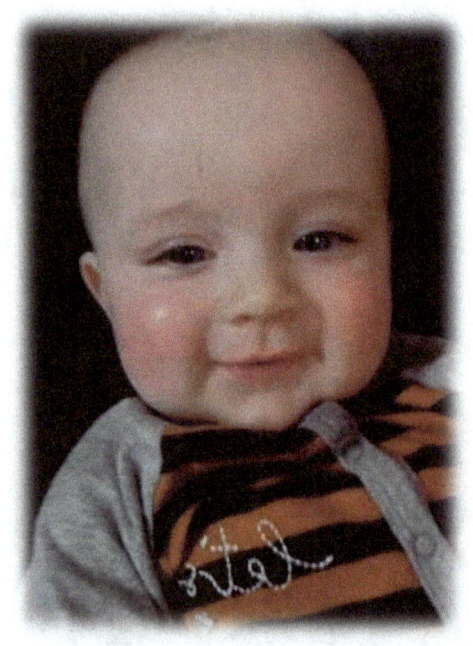

# This Book

*As You can see clear*
*I hold this Book dear*
*Please do not tear*

# Lacey

I was crazy
For a girl named Lacey
So I picker her a daisy

# Easter Bunny

*Honey Your so Funny
Dressed up as the
Easter Bunny*

# Grandchildren

*Grandchildren I love You*
*Each and Everyone*
*You bring joy a happiness*
*Like warmth from the sun*
**Dedicated to my Grand Children**

# Blessed

*I'm blessed*
*I'm gonna dress*
*My best*

# Story Told

*As I Grow old*
*My life is not on hold*
*My story needs to be told*

# Lighthouse

The lighthouse
Shines its light
So bright
So, the boats can see
In the foggy night

# Love Flows

As You smile
We talk a while
We're not in denial
As our love flows
Like rivers of
The Nile

# Paradise

I see it in Your eye's
Paradise is Yours and mine
To love and have
Good times

# The Dark

*I won't be afraid*
*Of the dark*
*I will keep You*
*In my heart*
*Even if were*
*Two world's a past*

# Honey's Bear's

The bear's climbing the tree's
Trying to take the sweet honey
From the Bee's

# Mother's Love

A mother's love
Safe in my arms
I will keep You from harm
Love You and keep You warm

# Nimm

My little dog Nimm
She was my shining light
She was smart and bright
And so full of life
I was blessed to have her in My life
I was sad when she went away
I miss her every day
**Dedicated to: Nimm**

# Paisley's Paws

Happy playful loving and sooth
By my side she always stood
Paisley's Paws
Were so wonderful faithful and true
I will forever Love You
**Dedicated to: Paisley**

# A Hurricane

*A hurricane*
*Brings a lot of rain*
*Destruction and pain*

# Keep You Near

As You weep
In a deep
Sleep
I keep You near
And take away Your fear

# Ukraine War

Death and destructions
The Earth scorched, burned, bombed
And scattered
Lives of love one's, family's and animals
Shattered
People lost and torn by a
Wickedness the world calls war
But it all is not gone
As the battle rages on
For the people of Ukraine shall
someday soon sing
And the bells of their freedom
Will always and forever ring
**Dedicated to: For the people of Ukraine**

## His Light

*I look at my life*
*And I wonder if I can make it right*
*God reminds me I'm doing all right*
*I see His light*
*I smile Bright*

# Left To Die

All I wanted was Your love

But Your love for me was lost

You left me to die

And I paid the cost

You sacrificed me

And I died tragedy

In Tennessee

Now I'm in Heaven with the Angels

Is where I will be

**Dedicated To: Lacey Ellen of Tennessee**

# A Better World

*I try not to cry sometimes*
*As I watch the news that arrives*
*Animals and people just trying to stay alive*
*The world is cruel sometimes*
*I pray for a better world*
*And to save lives*

# Ground Round

I went to town
To buy some Ground Round
It was 4.18 A Pound
I frowned
I wish the Price would Lower down

# Better Life

I packed the car
And grabbed my coat
Took our kids
And left a note
As I told my kids
It will be alright
Were headed out into the world
To have a better life

# Harmony

*I love You*
*And You love Me*
*Our baby makes Three*
*And We will live in harmony*

# Youthful Days

Sometimes
I wish I was still little
And still at play
But as we grow older
Our whole world has changed
But I'm still glad that I have
The memories of My youthful days

# *Fly Free*

*Fly on a breeze*
*Fly so free*
*The eagle fly's so beautifully*
*It's an amazing*
*Sight to see*

# Home of My Own

A home of My own
Some where I could dwell
Or put my stuff upon the shelves'
I could ware my pajama's
And sleep all day
Or stay up all night
And dance the night away
There's nothing like a place of My own
A place I could call home

# Flowers

The flower's that grow
Give a vibrant color of beauty
That shows

# We Were Young

*I miss those days*
*When We were young*
*We would laugh and have fun*
*Swimming in the river*
*Under the summer sun*

# Hoping To Mend

*Hoping Our Friendship*
*Don't End*
*I Send*
*Flowers to a Friend*
*Hoping to mend*

# *Say*

*I would just like to say*
*Let's all try to have a good day*
*As we work the day away*

# Zena

We go for walks everyday
But sometimes Zena's Paws
Lead Her Astray
Worn out and tired from our day
I pick Her up and carry Her
The rest of the way

**Dedicated to: Zena**

# So Long

*So Long*
*I'm gone*
*I'm moving on*

# This Book

*Beautiful Girl*
*As pretty as a pearl*
*You make my head swirl*
*Let's give it a whirl*

# My Little Dog

*As I sit by myself*
*With loneliness and despair*
*My little dog reminds me*
*That She is there*
*To comfort threw good times and bad*
*She is always there for me*
*Even when I'm feeling sad*

# Pure Bliss

*I miss Your Kiss*
*Your lips*
*Our pure*
*Bliss*

# My Dogs

*My little dogs*
*I'm glad I had them in my life*
*I hope to see them again one day*
*In the after life*

# Let's Mend

Let's mend
And spend
Time being
Friends

# Wallet

As I drove to town
I left my wallet at the house
I got a big frown
I had to turn around

# The Cat

The cat
He Lye's real still
Watching with a gaze,
His tall twitches
As he pounces
On his pray

# Wolves Call

*As darkness appears*
*And winter snows fall*
*I Love to hear*
*The beautiful sound of*
*The wolves call*

# Wolves Howl

*The night is bound*
*The wolves howl a beautiful sound*
*Until the morning comes around*

# As Darkness Falls

*Upon the night*
*The night owl*
*Is in flight*
*Under the beautiful*
*Moon light*

# Enter Peace

The grass blows in the breeze
There's tall giant beautiful tree's
The smell of wild flower's
Is in the air
A sense of enter peace is there

# Bird Song

The bird whistling
In the tree's
Carry's his tune
On a breeze
His music is a melody
In the air
A song of peace
Is there

# Heavenly Life

*If everyone shared compassion*
*To do what's right*
*Then the world we live in*
*Would be a heavenly life*

# Date

I took You on a date tonight
You smiled bright
As we danced under
The moon light

# Summer Day

On a summer day
The cat plays
While the sleeping dog Lay's
The rabbit gazes
As the birds
Fly away

# Shed of Light

*The moon gives a shed*
*Of light*
*As darkness falls*
*Upon the night*

# Tornado

*Pitter patter splash and clang*
*Lightning strikes and winds bang*
*The thunder roars*
*In the midst a tornado soar's*

# Fiery Love

*I feel so alive*
*With You by my side*
*We share a fiery Love*
*We can't deny*

# Massive storms

*Mother nature sometimes roar's*
*Bringing destructions*
*With massive storms*

# Living my Dream

I'm gonna Be as happy
As I can be
Living my dream
Bless it Be

# Chicken Meal

*Chicken is one of my favorite meals*
*I love it baked fried or grilled*

# Excuse Me

Excuse Me
I'm sorry I got in Your way
If I may say
Have a good day

# Animals of Nature

Wind brushing threw the trees
Birds soaring on a breeze
The wind whistles in the air
All the animals of nature live there

# A Glance

*As You gave me a glance*
*I was in a trance*
*I knew I had a chance*
*So, I asked You to dance*

# Open Range

*Grass growing on rolling hills*
*Cattle grazing on open fields*
*River's and streams it's like a dream*

# Sincere

*You have nothing to ever fear*
*As I hold you near*
*And tell You I love You my dear*
*I am forever sincere*

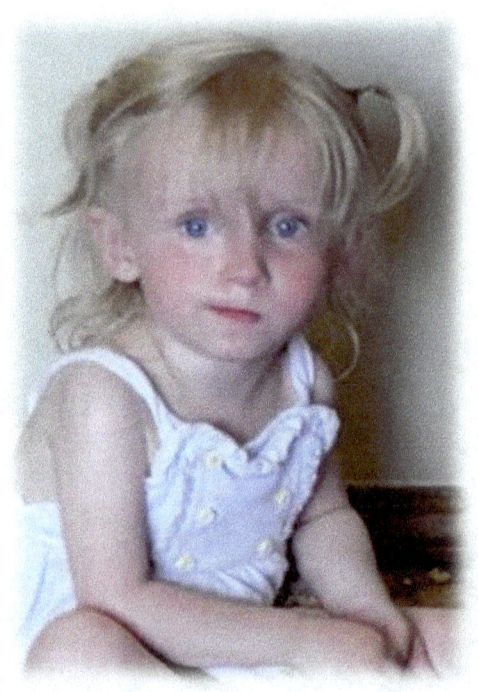

# Home Alaska

Alaska the place I call home
The place where berries
And wildflowers grow

# Night Away

*Today*
*The music plays*
*I wanna stay*
*And dance the*
*Night away*

# Stars Aline

The stars Aline
As our Two World's collide
Were put to the test
As we do Our very Best

# Mountain Top

I tripped over a rocl
I caught myself before I dropped
As I climbed over the treacherous
Mountain top

# America

America land of the free
Where I love to be
Happily, and share my dreams

# Beautiful World

As I stand hear quietly and breath
I can clearly see
The beautiful world
Like I've never seen

# Ton's of Fun

As we run
We begun
To have tons of fun
Under the sun

# The Eagle

*The Eagle soar's*
*To get His score*
*He's had a Good day*
*After he's gotten his pray*

# Animals

I love animals they bring
Joy. Love. Fun and cheer
And sooth my tear's

# More Than

*More than the great divide*
*The love I have for you*
*Will never die*

# A New Start

*Left in the dark*
*I had A broken heart*
*It felt Like I was falling apart*
*I lift my head up and do my part*
*And make way for a new start*

## *A Whisper*

*A whisper in your ear*
*The things You love to hear*
*I love You so much*
*I would follow You anywhere*

# You're The One

You're the one
And when You come around
I try not to act dumb
And when You talk to me
I trip over my own tongue
I know in my heart
You're truly the one

# Companion

Tears of joy, hopes, and fear's
Still together after all these years
A soft-spoken gentle nature
Like warmth from the sun
I knew from the beginning
That you were the one
So wonderful faithful and true
My dear companion I love You

# Belong

*Another day gone*
*I hold on*
*I stay strong*
*I know I belong*

## Compassion

Having compassion in the world
To better things
Having compassion for other people and animals
Will make Your heart sing

# Sleep Tight

*Turn off the light*
*You'll be all right*
*Sleep tight*
*Wake in the morning*
*Bright*

# Rain's

As the rains come pouring down
I love to hear the soothing and
Comforting sound

# Close To You

I feel close to You
I tell you what ever is on my mind
You listen with compassion
As I tell You how I feel Inside

# Seagull

As the seagull soar's
The ocean tide's
Wash sea shells
Upon the shores

# Prowl

The owl make's a shrill sound
As the wolves' howl
The bear goes on the prowl

# Time To Change

*A time of change is in the air*
*A new beginning is coming near*
*A sense of mystery is waiting for me there*

# *Cocoa*

*I remember December*
*When it was so cold*
*We would make hot cocoa*
*On or wood store*

# Good Live's

*God gave us Mother Earth*
*And Father sky*
*So, the people in the world*
*Could have good lives*

# Shine On

*Tall big short skinny of small*
*A women's beautiful glow*
*Will Shine On*

# Candle

A candle burns bright
And gives a vibrant
Glow of light
In the night

# The Sun

The sun shines down
Giving the earth a glow
And helps the plants trees grow

# Dancer

You jump and flip
With not a care in the world
You run like a breeze
And do it with ease
The way you dance
Is like a dream

# Wood Stove

*I love my old wood stove*
*It's easy to heat*
*Nice and toasty*
*And warms up my feet*

# Gone

*Where did I go wrong*
*I waited too long*
*The girl of my dreams*
*Is gone*

# Our Mind

Love laughter
Pain and tears
Music memories
Dreams and fears

# A Rose

I gave You a rose
I love You more than You know
From Your head to your toe's

## Never Part

*You're the only one that knows my heart*
*You knew it from the very start*
*That we will never part*
*I will love You always*
*From the bottom of my Heart*

# Summer Storms

Summer storms
The rains that pour
And the sound of
Rolling thunder roar

# Mosquitos

*As I go for walks during the day*
*I try to keep the mosquitos at bay*
*But pretty soon they swarm and bite*
*And I find myself running for my life*

# Smile

*I see You smile*
*As I'm standing in the Isle*
*I like Your wild style*
*So, we talked a while*

# Lightning Flash

*Rain pour's rolling thunder roar's*
*Snap crackle boom static electricity*
*And lightning flash*
*I find myself doing the hundred-yard dash*

# Heart Is True

Your eyes are blue
Your heart is true
No one could change
The way I feel
About You

# Love

As time passes on

My love for You will stay strong

It will never change and stay the same

So true the love from Me to You

## Peace And Beauty

I listen to the river

As it flows

And it starts to snow

There's a feeling of peace and beauty

That I now know

# *Find Love*

I will find love

As sure as the mysterious moon glows

As sure as the winter snows

Love will find me

# Precious Time

Precious time

Is yours and mine

Spend it well

And you will find

Love happiness

And good times

# Rise Up

Rise up for liberty and justice

Rise up for freedom and glory

Rise up for the occasion and celebration

## Cool Breeze

All the leave's

Have fallen off the tree's

Every thing is starting to freeze

The winter brings a cold breeze

# The Will

*Having the will to daily things*

*Having the will to keep or change things*

*Having the will means everything*

# *In My Life*

*A kiss so sweet*

*And smile so bright*

*I'm glad I found You*

*And have You in My life*

## *Forever*

*After everything We been through*

*Good or bad rich or poor*

*Long winters and summer storms*

*Forever true no one love's You as much*

*As I do*

## Favorite Songs

A new band is playing my favorite songs

Would You like to come along

It won't take too long

We better get gone

## My Devotion

Like water rippling across the ocean

Nothing is as pure as my devotion

Like ships at sea

We will always be together You and ME

# Blessed

Don't be depressed

Just do Your best

We are all blessed

And the rest

Will fall into place

## *It's Okay*

Ripped like a piece of paper

Broken like a piece of glass

I knew the love You had for me

Wouldn't last

It's okay Your gone

I've decided to move on

## Good Bye

I'm not good at goodbye's

I had the greatest time in My life

Having fun with You by my side

# Depression

Shunned and ignored

Not cared for anymore

Life is bleak

Depression sinks in deep

Shamed and blamed

Just want to be accepted the same

## Greatest Love

Open Your heart

And I will be true

I will give You Love

Like You Never knew

Just open Your heart to mine

And You will find

The greatest love

Of all time

# Mermaid

Beautiful mermaid

That swims in the sea

Saves another soul

From drowning at sea

# Days Pass On

As days pass on

I try to stay strong

I wonder what I did wrong

That made You want to sing a different song

The days are long

But I try to move on

# Glow Of Light

*The moons mysterious glow of light*

*Is the world's biggest night light*

## The Place

Home the place where I grew up

The place where I had all my

Childhood stuff

The place where I had family and friends

The place where I had good times

Well spent

# Smell Of Rain

Sound of River's flowing

Summer breeze blowing

Smell of rain in the air

Make me wanna stay there

# A Little Bark

I hear a noise in the dark

It was a little bark

I followed the sound and found

A little dog cold and all alone

Hungry and without a home

I took her in and warmed Her up

Gave her food and lots of love

Now she'll never be alone

I gave her a place to call home

# Son

God gave me the greatest gift in my life

The day I gave birth to a beautiful Son

In my life

Dedicated to My son

June 30-2022

# Shelter Animal

Animals at the shelter

Happy to be alive

Waiting to be adopted

And hoping there not passed bye

So, adopt a shelter animal

And give them a loving good life

# As You Cry

As You cry

You try to hide

Your lying eyes

You sigh

But I can see inside

You feel pain as rough as the

Ocean tide

## Voice Roar

Don't be silenced

Let your voice roar

And your heart will soar

And you will adore

The world

# Love Is Bright

As we sit under the moonlight

Our love is bright

It feels right

## I Will Be The One

When it's all said and done

I will be the one

As You cry and feel like You want to die

I will be there to help You strive and

Thrive and feel alive

I will be at Your side

To help You threw bad times

# Run

As we run into the night

Were living on the edge of our life

Looking for a future so bright

Sharing our loving light

# Poems

Alaska

Where my dreams come true

Writing different poems for you

## All Time

I'm there to have and hold

And grow old

I'm glad Your mine

I will love You for all time

## Gleam

Stand up and scream

And believe in your dreams

And let Your heart gleam

# Pass You By

*Clouds in my sky*

*The birds that fly*

*Don't let the world*

*Pass You by*

## Follow Your Dreams

*I remember when You followed Your dreams*

*Time did tell*

*You're doing so well*

# Being Blue

Tired of being blue

I need to see You

We can make it through

Our love can be true

## Smile Bright

Your life is a shining light

Like the stars at night

So, hold your head up tight

And smile bright

# Except Me

*By the way*

*I want You to stay*

*I pray You say*

*Yes, and except me the same*

## I Need You

I need You

I'm lonely and blue

I feel like I'm broken in two

When I don't have You

I will always love You

My heart is true

# Never Blue

Never blue

Sharing love with You

My dream has come true

# Mend

I try to pretend

But it seems to not end

I send a message of prayer

Oh, dear Lord help me mend

# Another Life

I know I met You

In another life

It feels so right

So, I asked You to be my wife

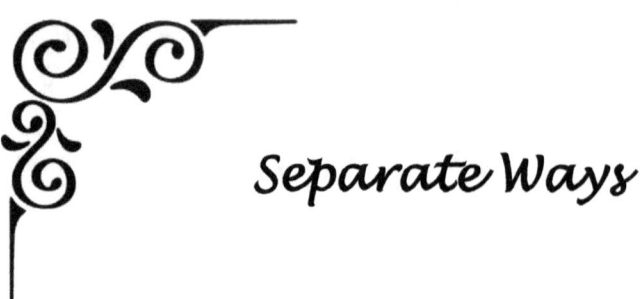

## Separate Ways

As We go Our separate ways

I just want to say

Neither one us is to blame

Neither one us need to feel shame

I will always love You the same

# *Remember*

*If You remember my dear*

*I will love You forever*

*And keep You near*

## On The Street

I feel sad for people living on the street

Having holes in their shoes of their feet

Being cold with nothing to eat

Having a hard time trying to find a seat

So, they could have a good night's sleep

I pray for them to have salvation and peace

# I'm Here

It's okay I'm here today

To take You away

With me to forever stay

And I will make You happy

Everyday

# Kind A Cold

I'm trying not to sound bold

But will You please kick up the wood stove

It's kind a cold

# On My Knee's

She's got me on my knee's

Asking Her Please

To forever be Mine

And share our dreams

## I'm Poor

I'm poor but I still adore

The finer things in life

That I could never afford

Which is a good thing otherwise I would probably

Hoard, oh thank the Lord

# My Clock

Bing Bang Bach

My Clock

Make's a weird

Knock

# Times Of War

I hate times of war that roar's

They need to restrain and be humane

Because the people of Ukraine

Don't need to feel anymore pain

**Dedicated to the People of Ukraine:**

# Cooking Pot

My favorite cooking pot

The one gramma bought

I made a pot of stew

For Me and You

## *Better Day*

I don't like to feel pain

Or shame and blame

It makes me feel like I'm wasting away

So, I tell myself to quit playing the game

And I walk away

And try to have a better day

# *Flashlight*

*Camping out at night*

*We would tell scary stories*

*And give each other a fright*

*With the flashlight*

# Embrace

I will never erase

The look You had on Your face

As I would chase

You around new place

And then we would embrace

# Pop Bottle's

When I was Young

I would collect soda Pop Bottle's

And get a refund

So, I could go buy bubble gum

## A Mess

I need to get dressed

My hair is a mess

I don't really obsess

But I try to look my best

# Share Our Life

I can't hide the feelings

I have inside

I want You by my side

So, I asked You to be my wife

And share Our life

# A Hole

I feel low

There's a hole

In my soul

Please don't go

# Always Love

Even though We are

Two worlds apart

I will always love You

Sweet heart

# Gravity

As gravity holds Me down

I feel like I'm going to drowned

I cry out loud

But no one hears my sound

So, I frown

And I pick myself up off the ground

# Picnic

There's no other place

That I would rather be

Then having a picnic with You

Under Our favorite tree

# Work

As I wake up and Rise

I clear my eyes

I don't waste anytime

I jump into my ride

And I fly

To work before the day passes by

## Summer Sun

I love to play

And have fun

Under the summer sun

Until the day is done

## Having Fun

I'm not the only one

Having fun

Dancing under the sun

I hope the day is never done

# rBreaking Hearts

I see You walk out the door

My mind can't take much more

Let's quit breaking each other's heart

We don't need to be apart

## Out Of Gas

On Our date tonight

We ran of gas under the moonlight

You got a fright

And turned on the head light

I told You it would be alright

I will hold You tight

And You smiled bright

# United States

*United States*

*Where I walk a free woman*

*I am so proud to walk upon*

*These Lands*

## Heart Ache

You give me a heartache

You're making it break

I can't see straight

I wake up late

I hate

Feeling this way

# A Good Man

With all that I know

And all that I am

I am a good man

I would love to take Your hand

And live off the land

# Recognize

My world was a storm

But You wouldn't recognize me any more

I'm doing great

I got a wife three kids and farm

And a loving dog with a lot of charm

# Soldier

He has to wait until he's a little older

His dream is to become a soldier

He has a plan

And wants to take a stand

And honor and protect his home land

# Married

Forever and ever

My love will be true

I so glad I married You

# Fire

I feel bad

When fire burns the land

All the animals and people

That perish makes me sad

# Typhoon

As the typhoon draws near

Rain and floods appear

Bringing destruction

That is hard to bare

# God Is Great

God is great

God is divine

God is here

For all mankind

## My Story

As I wait for My life to unfold

I'm scared of the unknown

And how my story will be told

And what it will show

But I would still like to know

# Dawn's Light

As the dawns light appears

A new day is here

To have and hold

Someone You love dear

# Floods

As the sky's go gray

A big storm is on its way

The rain starts to pour

And thunder starts to roar

The winds blow

And lightning flash

And flood water starts to splash

And everything starts to crash

And the people and animals try to get out fast

# Show Me Lord

Show Me Lord

Always keep me kind and caring

Until my time is done

# Another Tomorrow

As I left the town where I grew up

I had to leave some of my favorite stuff

All the stuff I cherished

I had to let perish

I feel sorrow

But I will return another tomorrow

Dedicated To: Myton Utah

## Share Memories

Me and My friend

Share memories

Of riding bikes

And climbing trees

And getting chased

By Honey Bee's

## Heaven Sent

It was worth it in the end

Because my heart needed to mend

I will never for get

That it was Heaven sent

# Best Love

Tired of waiting

For the next time

I will find a way

To make You mine

And we will share

The best love

Of all time

## Every Step

Every step I take

Will lead me to another place

I run with grace

As I chase

My dreams

I feel the embrace

# A Plan

I have a plan

To buy some land

And build a home

And grow vegetables of my own

A place for You and Me

To forever be

# Super Hero

If I was a super hero I would be

The greatest hero You have ever seen

I would fight fires crime and disease

We would never have wars

We would all be at peace

# River Of Love

Your kiss is like a whisper

That sends me shiver's

And I start to quiver

As You deliver

A river of love

## Beautiful Lands

Harmony and peace filled the air

With amazement I gazed upon the

Beautiful lands

That God made with a touch of his hand

# Hold On

*As I stand upon*

*I don't want to be gone*

*So I hold on*

## Love Is a Storm

Let's not yell I'm sure

Our love is a storm

So, I walk out the door

I don't want to hurt anymore

# As You walked by

And said hi

I almost cried

I miss You so dear

I had to wipe my tears

# Beauty We Hold

The beauty we hold

God's work so forever told

Keep it near

It is to hold forever dear

# Live Wire

She's a live wire

With a crazy style

And a perfect smile

## Sweet Story

I will always love You so

And You and I both know

As we grow old

We will have a sweet story told

# Forever Stand

God has a plan

For the people to forever stand

To cherish and protect His

Beautiful land

# White Owl

The white owl in flight

Trying to fulfill his appetite

Spots a mouse in the night

The mouse runs in fright

And the owl misses out on his bite

# Lonely Lover

*Lonely lover*

*You will find another*

*And they will be like no other*

*And You will love forever*

# Dark Clouds

As dark clouds form

The rain pours

Lightning flash looks formed

As another day approaches

With a summer storm

# Heart Of Gold

Heart of Gold

You would be well known

Threw the words You have shown

## Morning Dew

As long as I'm with You

We will always make it threw

Our love is as sweet

As the morning dew

# On My Feet

I'm on my feet again

I just needed time to mend

And console and heal my soul

# Next To Me

My life would be perfectly

If You would stand next to Me

And we had a family

And share Our life happily

# Hush Puppy

Hush puppy please don't cry

Someone will adopt You

And give You a good life

## Love Will Grow

I love You more than You know

Even when we are old

Our love will always grow

# Rain Drops

Rain drops from flowers that are there

Harmony and peace fill the air

A feeling of inner beauty is there

# Floods Draw Near

*Rains appear*

*And floods draw near*

*It's hard to stop my tears*

*As everything disappears*

# Lightning Strikes

Lightning strikes in the night

It lights up the sky's so bright

I hold on tight

As it flash's with an Eerie fright

# Have Fun

I wanna have fun

So, I jump and run

And play in the summer sun

# Grow

*As We both grow*

*You and I know*

*We will love each other so*

# Teddy Bear

*As You hold near*

*Your teddy bear*

*He takes away Your fear*

*As You wipe your tears*

# The Dawn's Light

The moonlight was glowing bright

In the still of night

The white owl had taken flight

The wolves' putting up a fight

To protect their young from

A predators fright

Animals of the night

Waiting for the dawn's light

## Alaska The Place

Alaska the place I love to be

You've gotta' see it to believe

Water rippling across the ocean

People are kind and caring and give

Great devotion

Rivers and streams

It like a dream

Beautiful lands and animals of nature

Perfect for a tourist vacationer

## Games And Lies

You can't hide Your games and lies

So why try and mess up other people's lives

Instead, you should do what is right

And share Your kindness and loving light

And You will have a future so bright

And in return people will give You

Caring and kindness in your life

# Sunsets

Everyday

God puts on a display

For the whole world to see

His beautiful scenes

Sunsets beauty forever seen

# Snow Fall

Getting A cold chill

Sliding down hills

Having a ball

As blankets of snow fall

Having snow ball fights

One and all

# Move To the Beat

In the summer heat

My feet move to the beat

As I dance on the street

# Love Flows Free

Love will find Me

And I will be

Forever happy

As my love flows free

# Poodle Puppy

I got a poodle puppy

She was a little Tuffy

I named her Muffy

She was soft and fluffy

# *A Lot Better*

*If We all*

*Worked together*

*The world*

*Would be*

*A lot better*

## Celtic Music

*I love Celtic Music*

*It soothes and consoles*

*And helps to heal*

*My soul*

# The Sun

The sun shines down

Giving the Earth a glow

If shines down and helps

The plants and trees grow

# Dreams Don't Die

Dreams don't die

So, strive and thrive

And bring your dreams to life

And shine bright

Like the stars at night

# God's Work

*All of God's work*

*So lovely and true*

*I'm so glad He made You*

# Aurora Lights

Aurora lights

Colored bright

Shine in the Alaska night

# Our Life

Who knew

That I would marry You

And our Life would be true

## Motion

Your love is like a

Magic potion

You give me such

Loving devotion

And it sets me in

Motion

## See Threw

I look at You

And I see threw

Your love is true

My world is never Blue

# Don't Walk Away

I need You

Please don't walk away

You're not the one to blame

I just want You to except me the same

# Stay

*It's okay*

*I will wait for another day*

*For You to say*

*Yes, I can stay*

# Salmon

River's Like A Dream

As The Bear's Tag Team

The Salmon Swimming

Up Stream

## *I Pray*

*The words I Say*

*Every day*

*As I Pray*

*For every one*

*To have A Good Life*

*In the World*

*We Stay*

# Angelique's

Antique's

And

Boutique

Sounds

Unique

# Glorify

It is No Surprise

Miracles Have Happened

In Front of my Eye's

And I Rise

And I Glorify

Towards the Sky

# So Bold

I Stare in your Eye's so Bold

And I wonder what you Hold

in Your Life you Have not Told

# Better

On my Feet Again

Better than I've ever been

All I needed was a Little

Time to Mend

## I Cry

The Love I Have For You will Never Die

I Cry

And say my Good Bye

As you are lifted towards the sky

# Pretty Eye's

*I Hold You so True*

*Pretty Eye's of Blue*

*Your Love is A Magic Brew*

## Dust From A Star

Here we are Looking

From A far

Dust from A star

Sharing our Love and Heart

# Cauldron

*In Her Cauldron Of Blue*

*She Makes Her Magic Brew*

*A Hot Pot Of Beef Stew*

# A Soldier's Storm

A Soldier's Storm

Broken And Torn

By A Thorn

Of War

# Ghouls Of The Night

The witch is in Flight

While the Ghosts scare with all there might

Dracula is on the prowl to get a Bite

Frankenstein is A scary Sight

The where wolf Give's A Howling Fright

As we run From The ghouls of the Night

**Dedicated to : Lacey**

# Dreaming On A Star

Here we Are

Looking from a far

Dreaming on A Star

# Freedom Forever

Soldier's Ban Together

To Fight for Freedom

Forever

# Worth

*Your Life*

*is worth*

*Being On*

*Earth*

# You To Hold

I Have Poem's

In my Soul

To Be Told

For You To Hold

# Dance Around

As I Dance Around

To A Beautiful Sound

Music in My Ear

Melody's I Love To Hear

# North Star

I Drive in My Car

Driving very Far

Following The North Star

Cause I wanna Be

Where You Are

# Splashed

I woke Up To The Sound

Of A Storm

I Looked out my Window

As the Thunder Roared

I Got Dressed Rel Fast

As The Lightning Flashed

I Hurried And Ran Across The Floor

As the Rain's Started To Pour

Went our my Front Door

And Rolled Up my Window's with A dash

Before My Seats Got Splashed

# I Lost You

*My world is Blue*

*My Fear came True*

*The day I Lost You*

## Rock Star

Always in a New Car

Everyone knows who you are

You're a Famous Rock Star

Playing Your Beautiful Guitar

Down At the Local Bar

# I Survive

I Revive

And I strive

I Survive

And I make it out

Alive

# Clam's

I Take You By The Hand

And we run through the sand

Under the sun getting Tan

And digging up clams

# *Try*

*All we can do is try*

*And get by*

*And be kind*

*In a world we need to*

*Survive*

# Clam's

I Take You By The Hand

And we run through the sand

Under the sun getting Tan

And digging up clams

# A Dove

A dove

Flying Above

The world

it Love's

# Gold Dust

Digging in the Earth's crust

Through the rocks I Bust

On my search for Gold Dust

# Furry Friend

A Furry Friend

Till The End

Animals Are Angels

Hiding in Plain Sight

Giving A Loving Light

# Fire Flies

Enchanting sight

Fire flies Glow of Light

Shining in the Night

# She

She Has

Lips Red As A Rose

A Cute Little Button Nose

Teeth Perfect Pearly White

Beautiful Eye's that Shined Bright

And A Smile that was Kissed

By The Sun's Light

# Spring

The Freeze is Gone

Spring has come along

The Plants and Flowers

Are Growing Strong

As Spring Plays A Beautiful Song

# Haley's Comet

A Different Color in the Night

A Long Tail Of Streaming Light

What A Beautiful Sight

Haley's Comet So Bright

# Harp

Gentle Song of A Broken

Heart And Love And Art

Strumming the Strings

Of A Beautiful

Harp

# No Nuclear War

We Need To Think

Before People And Animals

Become extinct

With Just A Blink

Everything would Be Ruined

From shore to shore

Say No To Nuclear War

Because We Need The World

We Love And Adore

# Dice

You came Around

And lay your money Down

And Listen to the Sound

As You Roll the Dice

Hoping to Win the Round

# The Lord Loves Us

A Glorifying Sight

The Lord Loves Us

with All His Might

He gives a guiding light

So our Future can Be Bright

## Day We Met

My mind was set

And I will Never Regret

Or ever forget

The day we met

# The Witch

Dancing with Her Broom in the Night

Around A Fire So Bright

She takes off in flight

Under the Beautiful moon light

# Talking To You

Talking To You made my day

And ever though we are mile's away

I just want to say

Don't worry for me

I Will Be Okay

# Never Broken

I will Never Be Broken

My Arms Will Always Be Open

To Care And Show

My Love will Always Grow

For The World I Know


**Dedicated to: Jessica**

# Shall Pass

When You're Having a Bad Day

I would Just Like To Say

Everything will be Okay

The Bad Will Not Last

This to Shall Pass

# God Walks Beside Me

Sometimes I am sad

Some People Make Me Feel Bad

But I still Try my Best

Because I know I am Blessed

For God walks Beside Me

Through Every Test

# White Red and Blue

I Love You True

White Red and Blue

A Bouquet of Flower's

I Picked For You

# A Child's Smile

A Childs Smile

So Bright

Is a Parents

Loving Light

## Clover

A Sign

To Be Kind

A Four Leaf Clover

Love the World Over

# River of Gold

The water is cold

But a pan I hold

As I sift the River

of Gold

# Glacier Water

Alaska River's of Blue

Glacier Water

Pure and True

What A Beautiful view

# Treasure of Gold

I want You to Know

You're the One I hold

Your my Treasure of Gold

# Worth

*Your Life*

*is Worth*

*Being On*

*Earth*

# The Witch

Dancing with her Broom in the Night

Around a Fire so Bright

She Takes Off in Flight

Under the Beautiful Moonlight

# Heavy

Do not Be Bind

Leave what is heavy behind

And you will find

The world can be kind

# Forget Me Not

Forget me Not

SO I bought

You Flowers for the thought

# A Soldier's Storm

A Soldier's Storm

Broken And Torn

By A Thorn

Of War

## I Pray

The words I say

Everyday

As I Pray

For Everyone

To have a Good Life

in the World

We Stay

# Showing Beauty and Love

The Heaven's Above

Are Like a Whisper

From A Dove

Showing Beauty and Love

# My Devotion

Like water rippling across the ocean

Nothing is as pure as my devotion

Like ships at sea

We will always be together You and ME

# SHE

She Has

Lips Red As A Rose

A Cute Little Button Nose

Teeth perfect Pearly White

Beautiful Eyes that shined Bright

And A Smile That was Kissed

By The Sun's Light

# Talking To You

Talking To You Made My Day

And Even Though We Are Miles Away

I Just Wont To Say

Don't Worry For Me

I Will Be Okay

# I Cry

The Love I Have For You will Never Die

I Cry

And say my goodbye

As You Are Lifted Towards The Sky

# WORTH

*Your Life*

*Is Worth*

*Being on*

*Earth*

www.ingramcontent.com/pod-product-compliance
Lightning Source LLC
LaVergne TN
LVHW021956060526
838201LV00048B/1585